You Made Me

You Made Me

by Erin Minta Maxfield-Steele

RESOURCE *Publications* • Eugene, Oregon

YOU MADE ME

Copyright © 2020 Erin Minta Maxfield-Steele. All rights reserved. Except for brief quotations in critical publications or reviews, no part of this book may be reproduced in any manner without prior written permission from the publisher. Write: Permissions, Wipf and Stock Publishers, 199 W. 8th Ave., Suite 3, Eugene, OR 97401.

Resource Publications
An Imprint of Wipf and Stock Publishers
199 W. 8th Ave., Suite 3
Eugene, OR 97401

www.wipfandstock.com

PAPERBACK ISBN: 978-1-5326-8479-1
HARDCOVER ISBN: 978-1-5326-8496-8
EBOOK ISBN: 978-1-5326-8497-5

Manufactured in the U.S.A. 05/19/20

Scripture quoted by permission. All scripture quotations are taken from the NET Bible® copyright ©1996–2016 by Biblical Studies Press, L.L.C. All rights reserved.

Dedication: To all those whose bodies have been judged or rejected, mislabeled, misused, or misunderstood. To all whose bodies have held the experiences of struggle and oppression, liberation and joy, pain and strength.

To the little one we never held and to the little one being woven within me.
To Allyn—my partner, companion, ally, and love. EMS

Preface

This book is an invitation for all of us to think about our earliest moments. I hope that these words and images will open a door to a greater sense of embodied spirituality, both for you and for the young one you share it with. These particular lines of scripture hold deep meaning for me and they have informed my understanding of God and myself throughout my life. However, these same lines are frequently used with the intent to alienate and shame women faced with the difficult choices that pregnancy can bring. In light of this, I feel compelled to state explicitly that I do not give permission for any part of this work to be used to alienate, shame, or malign. My sincere hope is that this book will be a blessing. EMS

Certainly you made my **mind**
and heart;
you wove me together
in my mother's womb.
You knew me thoroughly;
my bones were not hidden from you,
when I was made in secret
and
sewed together
in the depths of the earth.

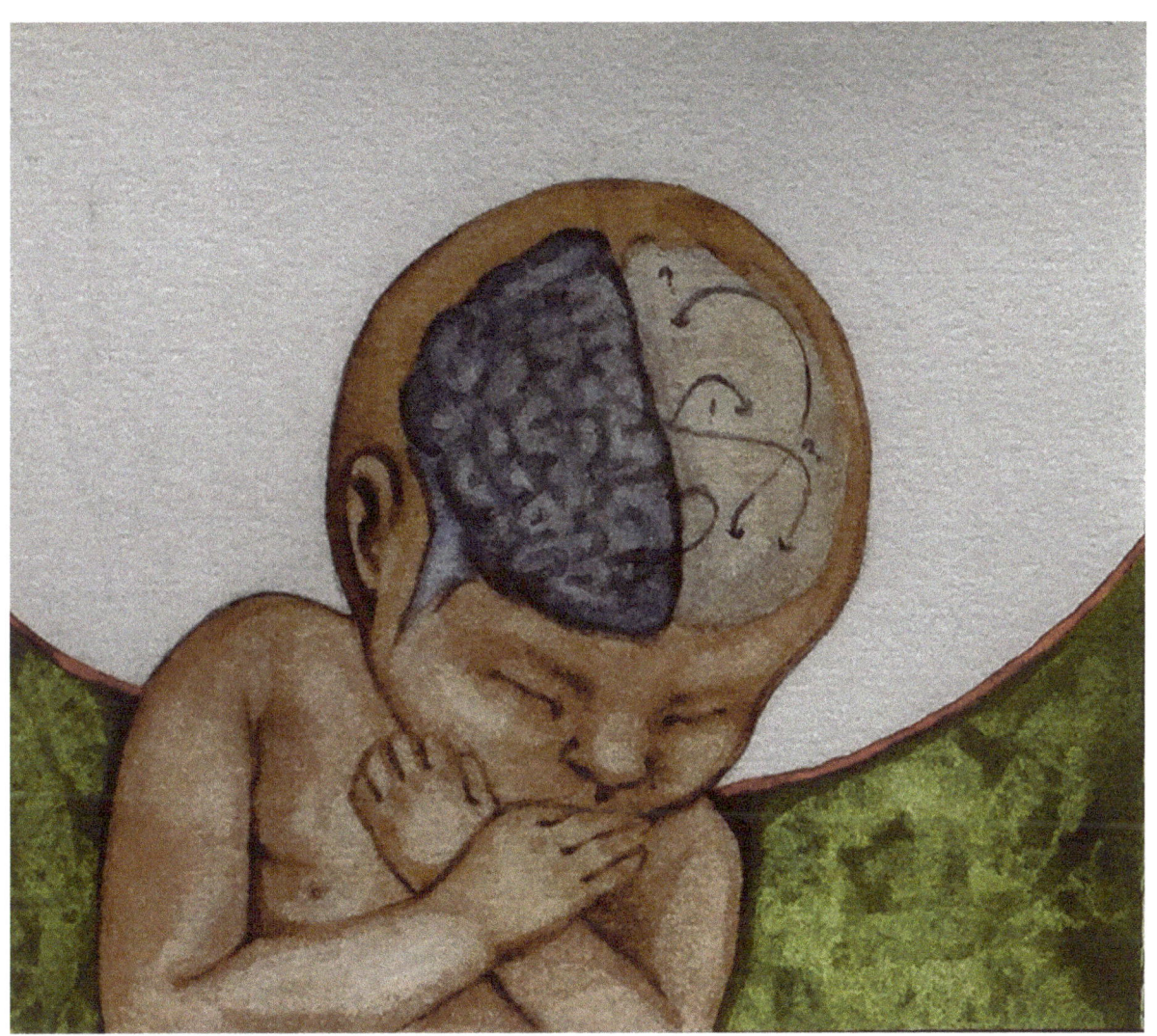

Certainly you made
my mind and **heart**;
you wove me together in my
mother's womb.
You knew me thoroughly; my bones
were not hidden from you,
when I was made
in secret
and sewed together in the depths of the earth.

Certainly you
made my mind and heart;
you wove me together in my
mother's womb. You knew me
thoroughly; my bones were not
hidden from you,
when I was made
in secret
and sewed together in the depths
of the earth.

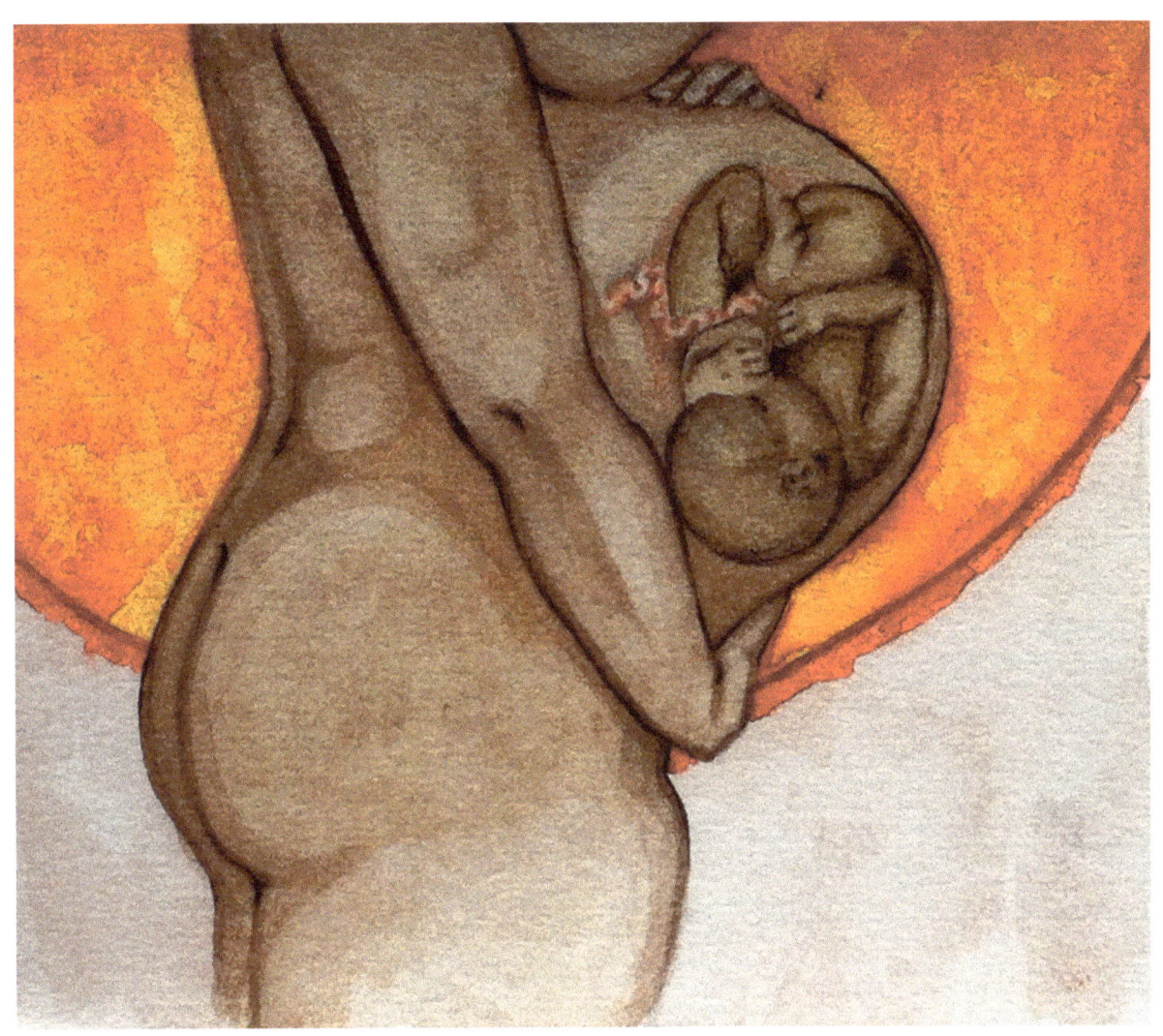

Certainly
you made my mind and heart;
you wove me together
in my mother's womb.
You
knew me thoroughly;
my bones were not hidden from you,
when I was made in secret
and sewed together in the depths
of the earth.

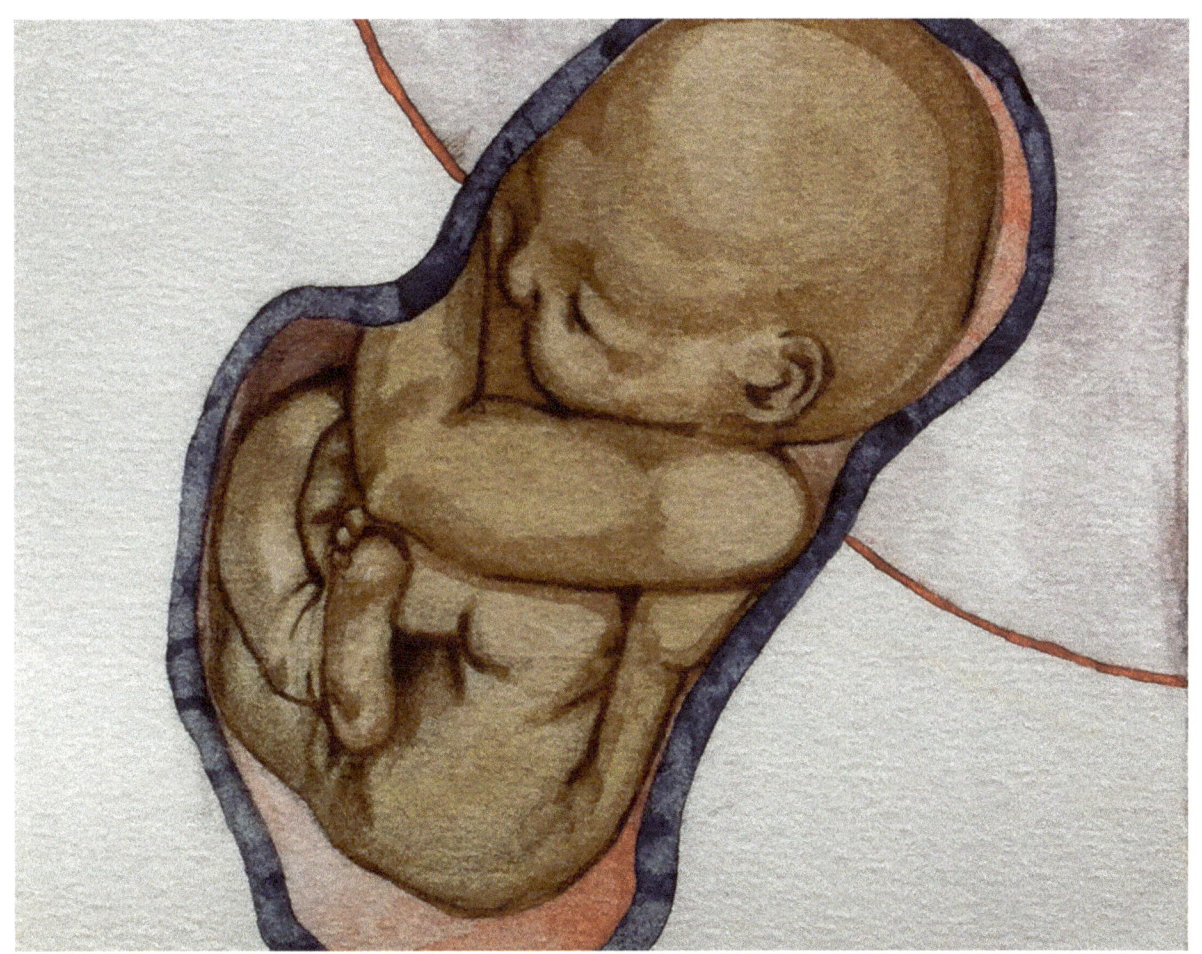

Certainly you made my mind and heart;

you wove me together in my mother's womb.

You knew me thoroughly;

my bones were not hidden

from you, when I was made

in secret

and sewed together

in the **depths**

of the earth.

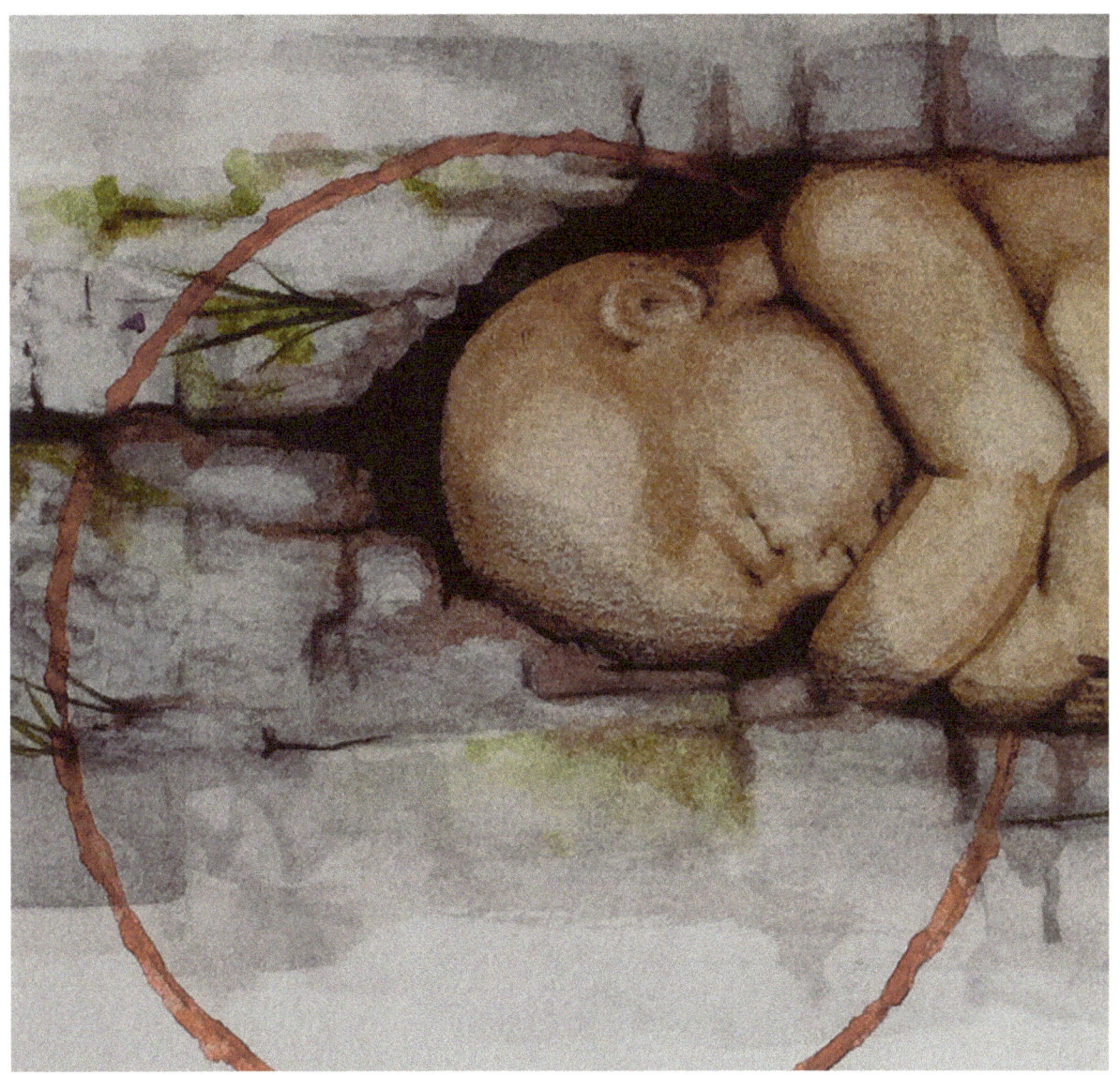

∼